WE NEED A

DEPARTMENT OF

PEACE

EVERYBODY'S BUSINESS, NOBODY'S JOB

COMPILED AND EDITED BY

WILLIAM L. BENZON

We Need a Department of Peace: Everybody's Business, Nobody's Job

Published by Wheatmark®
1760 East River Road, Suite 145
Tucson, Arizona 85718 USA
www.wheatmark.com

ISBN: 978-1-62787-430-4 (paperback)
ISBN: 978-1-62787-431-1 (ebook)
LCCN: 2016943618

Contents

Prologue:
War Is Not a Natural Disaster

Mary Liebman

The human race knows a lot about how to make war. We should: we've been doing it since biblical times. Experts define "war" as any conflict in which the dead number more than 3000 people. Below that number—by revolution, insurrection, armed exploration, native uprising, clan feud, violent strikes, lynching, riot, excessive partisanship of soccer fans, or plain personal murderousness—none of that counts until more than 3000 people have been slaughtered. Then it gets in the record books as a war. Disregarding our barbarian ancestors, the Attilas and Genghis Khans for whom war was a way of life; overlooking two centuries of carnage in nine Crusades, and the Hundred Years' War, which occupied France and England for 115 years, just looking at the world since Columbus discovered America, we find that the world has been at peace less than half the time, and the wars are getting bigger and worse.

Out of this collective experience with war, we've learned how to do it. Homer left notes. We have the memoirs of generals and statesmen from Caesar down to modern times to guide us. There are textbooks to study. And almost everyone in government has served in the armed forces or some other war-connected duty. They understand it.

By contrast, what do any of us know about how to make peace? Nobody has ever done it. Until Hiroshima, few people talked very seriously about doing it. The Bomb changed things forever. We

1

began to realize that no nation would ever again fight through to glorious victory.

The celebrations, the cheering crowds in Times Square, the church bells ringing, and the bands playing—those are sounds that belong to history. They will never be heard again at the end of any war, anywhere, by anybody. So while we are not better men than our ancestors, and maybe not much smarter, we are faced with the *necessity* of making peace—and nobody knows how.

Well, let's start with what we do know. In any public undertaking, from building a dam to putting a man on the moon, we start by hiring somebody to be in charge. We give him an office, a staff, a desk, a typewriter, a telephone. We give him a budget. We say, "Begin." It may come as something of a shock to realize that in this vast proliferating federal bureaucracy, there is no one in charge of peace. There is nobody who goes to an office in Washington and works nine-to-five for peace, unhampered by any other consideration or responsibility. [...]

War is not a natural disaster. It is a manmade disaster, directed and carried out by ordinary people, who are hired and paid by other ordinary people, to make war. It will stop when ordinary people decide that, whatever satisfactions and rewards war may have offered in the past, the risk is now too high and the return too low. If you are ready to invest in a new and exciting American enterprise, you can start by spending an hour telling your congressman why you want a Department of Peace.

⎯⎯≫◦◦◦≪⎯⎯

Mary Liebman published these words on the first two pages of the February 1973 issue of *PAX*, the newsletter for the Council for a

Department of Peace (CODEP). She had been honing this message for two years and would continue for three more. We note that back then it was true: as she said, "[A]lmost everyone in government has served in the armed forces or some other war-connected duty." That's no longer true. Conscription ended in 1973, with the eventual result that most people in government are too young to have faced the military draft or to have friends and relatives who did.

What's in This Pamphlet?

Bill Benzon

In the current political climate in the United States, where the nation seems trapped in war enterprises that are vaguely defined, never-ending, and futile, we need to remind ourselves that throughout much of the twentieth century, revulsion against and opposition to war was widespread. The First World War, known at the time as the Great War and even "the war to end all wars," killed and maimed so many that in 1928 the United States, along with many other nations, forswore the use of war in the General Treaty for Renunciation of War as an Instrument of National Policy, informally known as the Kellogg-Briand Pact. Alas, there has been a lot of backsliding.

Still, the Vietnam War provoked such outrage within the United States that citizen protests forced an end to the war. What is not so well-known—and this is the central message of this pamphlet—is that:

> *Widespread sentiment once existed for a department of peace within the United States. It was a mainstream political idea.*

In showing what active citizens were able to put on the national agenda, this pamphlet is both an argument and a handbook for creating a Department of Peace in the federal government of the United States. The central argument is simply that peace is not only morally right, but it is a practical necessity, as Mary Liebman's prologue states. The many ecological problems

5

humankind now faces cannot be resolved if we squander our lives and resources in warfare. Charlie Keil gives a succinct account these and other issues in "Waging Peace," the next to last chapter in the pamphlet.

One of the country's Founding Fathers, Benjamin Rush, was the first to argue for a department of peace in a pamphlet Benjamin Banneker published in 1793. His point was that we needed a focal point for peace planning and activity *within* government. We have reproduced that pamphlet in full and added a few comments on it.

That is followed by "Why a Department of Peace?" by distinguished historian Frederick L. Schuman. Schuman offers arguments for a department of peace and reviews the twentieth-century history of legislative efforts at creating a peace department starting with the 74th Congress in 1935 and continuing through to the 91st Congress in 1969. This was originally published in pamphlet form by Another Mother for Peace, an organization created in 1967 at the height of the Vietnam War. The organization attracted the widespread support of figures in the entertainment industry, including Donna Reed, Debbie Reynolds, Paul Newman, Joanne Woodward, and Dick Van Dyke.

Another Mother for Peace passed the baton to an organization that was founded as the Peace Act Advisory Council (PAAC) and then became the Council for a Department of Peace (CODEP). The chapter "Peace Is Everybody's Business; Nobody's Job" discusses that effort and is based on newsletters written by Mary Liebman. It covers legislation introduced in the 91st, 92nd, 93rd, and 94th Congresses ending in 1977. All these twentieth-century efforts had bipartisan support in Congress.

After we review the work of PAAC and CODEP, we have Charlie Keil's chapter, "Waging Peace," and we conclude with a short "Resolution for a Department of Peace," also by Keil. An appendix lists some currently active peace organizations along with contact information.

A Plan of a Peace-Office
for the United States

Benjamin Rush

Among the defects which have been pointed out in the Federal Constitution by its antifederal enemies, it is much to be lamented that no person has taken notice of its total silence upon the subject of an office of the utmost importance to the welfare of the United States, that is, an *office* for promoting and preserving perpetual *peace* in our country.[1]

It is to be hoped that no objection will be made in the establishment of such an office, while we are engaged in a war with the Indians, for as the *War-Office* of the United States was established in the *time of peace*, it is equally reasonable that a *Peace-Office* should be established in the *time of war*.

The plan of this office is as follows:

I.   Let a Secretary of the Peace be appointed to preside in this office, who shall be perfectly free from all the present absurd and vulgar European prejudices upon the subject of government; let him be a genuine republican and sincere Christian, for the principles of republicanism and Christianity are no less friendly to universal and perpetual peace than they are to universal and equal liberty.

II.   Let a power be given to this Secretary to establish and maintain free-schools in every city, village, and township of the United States; and let him be made responsible for the talents, princi-

---

[1]   This text is taken from Benjamin Rush, *Essays, Literary, Moral and Philosophical*, 2nd ed. (Philadelphia: Thomas and William Bradford, 1806), 183–88.

ples, and morals of all his schoolmasters. Let the youth of our country be carefully instructed in reading, writing, arithmetic, and in the doctrines of a religion of some kind: the Christian religion should be preferred to all others; for it belongs to this religion exclusively to teach us not only to cultivate peace with men, but to forgive, nay more—to love our very enemies. It belongs to it further to teach us that the Supreme Being alone possesses a power to take away human life, and that we rebel against his laws, whenever we undertake to execute death in any way whatever upon any of his creatures.[2]

III. Let every family in the United States be furnished at the public expense, by the Secretary of this office, with a copy of an American edition of the BIBLE. This measure has become the more necessary in our country, since the banishment of the bible, as a school-book, from most of the schools in the United States. Unless the price of this book be paid for by the public, there is reason to fear that in a few years it will be met with only in courts of justice or in magistrates' offices; and should the absurd mode of establishing truth by kissing this sacred book fall into disuse, it may probably, in the course of the next generation, be seen only as a curiosity on a shelf in a public museum.

IV. Let the following sentence be inscribed in letters of gold over the doors of every State and Court house in the United States.

THE SON OF MAN CAME INTO THE WORLD,
NOT TO DESTROY MEN'S LIVES,
BUT TO SAVE THEM.

---

[2]   This certainly sounds like a call to the Buddhist to "do no harm" and a vegetarian lifestyle!

V.   To inspire a veneration for human life, and an horror at the shedding of human blood, let all those laws be repealed which authorize juries, judges, sheriffs, or hangmen to assume the resentments of individuals and to commit murder in cold blood in any case whatever. Until this reformation in our code of penal jurisprudence takes place, it will be in vain to attempt to introduce universal and perpetual peace in our country.

VI. To subdue that passion for war, which education, added to human depravity, have made universal, a familiarity with the instruments of death, as well as all military shows, should be carefully avoided. For which reason, militia laws should every where be repealed, and military dresses and military titles should be laid aside: reviews tend to lessen the horrors of a battle by connecting them with the charms of order; militia laws generate idleness and vice, and thereby produce the wars they are said to prevent; military dresses fascinate the minds of young men, and lead them from serious and useful professions; were there no *uniforms*, there would probably be no armies; lastly, military titles feed vanity, and keep up ideas in the mind which lessen a sense of the folly and miseries of war.

VII. In the last place, let a large room, adjoining the federal hall, be appropriated for transacting the business and preserving all the records of this *office*. Over the door of this room let there be a sign, on which the figures of a LAMB, a DOVE, and an OLIVE BRANCH should be painted, together with the following inscriptions in letters of gold:

PEACE ON EARTH—GOOD-WILL TO MAN.
AH! WHY WILL MEN FORGET THAT
THEY ARE BRETHREN?

Within this apartment let there be a collection of ploughshares and pruning-hooks made out of swords and spears; and on each of the walls of the apartment, the following pictures as large as the life:

1. A lion eating straw with an ox, and an adder playing upon the lips of a child.
2. An Indian boiling his venison in the same pot with a citizen of Kentucky.
3. Lord Cornwallis and Tippoo Saib, under the shade of a sycamore-tree in the East Indies, drinking Madeira wine together out of the same decanter.
4. A group of French and Austrian soldiers dancing arm and arm, under a bower erected in the neighborhood of Mons.
5. A St. Domingo planter, a man of color, and a native of Africa, legislating together in the same colonial assembly.[3]

To complete the entertainment of this delightful apartment, let a group of young ladies, clad in white robes, assemble every day at a certain hour, in a gallery to be erected for the purpose, and sing odes, and hymns, and anthems in praise of the blessings of peace.

One of these songs should consist of the following lines.

> Peace o're the world her olive wand extends,
> And white-rob'd innocence from heaven descends;
> All crimes shall cease, and ancient frauds shall sail,
> Returning justice lifts aloft her scale.

---

[3]   Remember that in Rush's time there were wars between the United States and the American Indians, between the Britain and Tippo Sahib, between the planters of St. Domingo and their African slaves, and between France and the emperor of Germany.

In order more deeply to affect the minds of the citizens of the United States with the blessings of peace, by contrasting them with the evils of war, let the following inscriptions be painted upon the sign, which is placed over the door of the War Office.

1. An office for butchering the human species.
2. A Widow and Orphan making office.
3. A broken bone making office.
4. A Wooden leg making office.
5. An office for creating public and private vices.
6. An office for creating public debt.
7. An office for creating speculators, stock Jobbers, and Bankrupts.
8. An office for creating famine.
9. An office for creating pestilential diseases.
10. An office for creating poverty, and the destruction of liberty, and national happiness.

In the lobby of this office let there be painted representations of all the common military instruments of death, also human skulls, broken bones, unburied and putrefying dead bodies, hospitals crowded with sick and wounded Soldiers, villages on fire, others in besieged towns eating the flesh of their children, ships sinking in the oceans, rivers dyed in blood, and extensive plains without a tree or fence, or any other object, but the ruins of deserted farm houses.

Above this group of woeful figures,—let the following words be inserted, in red characters to represent human blood,

"NATIONAL GLORY."

Comments on
Benjamin Rush's Proposal

Bill Benzon

Benjamin Rush was a Philadelphia physician, founder of Dickinson College, the father of American psychiatry, an abolitionist, member of the Continental Congress, and a signer of the Declaration of Independence. Benjamin Banneker published the essay in the 1793 edition of his well-known almanac and then later in a collection of Rush's essays. It is an interesting and curious document, with an allegorical aspect that identifies sources of conflict that remain with us to this day.

Rush imagines that the department would be able to transact its business in a single large room "adjoining the federal hall." The world was much smaller then than it is now, and so a larger portion of that world's business could be encompassed within a single room. Rush is quite particular about the appointments of this room, suggesting that it house "a collection of ploughshares and pruning-hooks made out of swords and spears."

The allusion is biblical, of course (Isaiah 2:3–4). Rush also directed that each family in the country be provided with a Bible at government expense. We are still in dire need of moral guidance, though it is by no means obvious that the Bible is the best source of it. What would Rush think of the Dalai Lama, Mahatma Gandhi, or Pope Francis?

Rush also specifies that the walls of this office have large allegorical paintings on them. Thus the room itself is designed to inspire its inhabitants in their work. One of these paintings is to depict "an Indian boiling his venison in the same pot with a citizen of Kentucky." Did Rush have any sense that war with the Indians would continue for a century—the Wounded Knee Massacre was in 1890—and that relations between them and their conquerors would remain fraught to this day?

Another painting was to depict "Lord Cornwallis and Tippoo Saib, under the shade of a sycamore-tree in the East Indies, drinking Madeira wine together out of the same decanter." That of course depicts the British in India, who ruled there until 1947, when India became independent and partitioned into two states, India and Pakistan. The Tipu Sultan ruled the Kingdom of Mysore in southern India and was thus a Muslim ruler in a Hindu land.[4] If Cornwallis and the Sultan had been able to make peace, well, what then? It was only a painting—and not even one that had been executed—but the allegorical extension of its subject identifies what remains a vexatious knot of conflicts. If India can make its democracy work, that will be glorious. But what of the spiraling toxicity of the dance between death drones from the skies and Islamic extremism?

And then there's the painting depicting "a group of French and Austrian soldiers dancing arm and arm, under a bower erected in the neighborhood of Mons." According to the Wikipedia the Battle of Mons marked the British entry into the First World War."[5] And that particular conflict, among the French, the Germans, and the British, just got worse in the middle of the century, where it sucked half the world into a maelstrom of violence.

---

[4]   For basic information, consult the Wikipedia entry: https://en.wikipedia.org/wiki/Tipu_Sultan

[5]   See Wikipedia: https://en.wikipedia.org/wiki/Battle_of_Mons.

In the subjects he chose for these three paintings, Rush identified knots of sociocultural violence that remain with us to this day. We're not talking about violence in the abstract, but violence in specific historical situations that have not damped out but have simply changed shape and form. A fourth painting was to depict "a St. Domingo planter, a man of color, and a native of Africa, legislating together in the same colonial assembly." Santo Domingo is still in trouble[6]—trouble rooted in its colonial past.

Rush would no doubt have been pleased that men and women "of color" eventually came to legislative power in America and that a black man has become President of the United States. The situation of Africa, however, is a mess—some of it a legacy of colonialism, some the result of current exploitation by powerful interests both East and West, and most of it resting squarely in the laps of people who have to figure out how to survive and thrive in the world they've got.

As, indeed, must all of us.

But there was more to Rush's vision for the office. He also wanted the workers to be inspired by music sung by "young ladies, clad in white robes" who would "sing odes, and hymns, and anthems in praise of the blessings of peace." This was to be daily.

I have two reactions to this. On the one hand, I think of videos I've seen of Japanese workers doing calisthenics on the job; it's healthy and builds team spirit. I also think of 1985's "We Are the World," where a "supergroup"—Michael Jackson, Willie Nelson, Lionel Riche, Stevie Wonder, Dianna Ross, Paul Simon, Cyndi

---

[6]   For example, Joshua Jelly-Schapiro, "Waiting to be Deported in Santo Domingo," *The New Yorker* (June 27, 2015): http://www.newyorker.com/news/news-desk/waiting-to-be-deported-in-santo-domingo.

Lauper, and others—raised millions of dollars for humanitarian aid in Africa.[7]

It's anyone's guess what Rush would think of that music, but I can't help but think that a dialectical synthesis of such music with daily calisthenics would be good for anyone's soul.

There's more to Rush's proposal than these "symbolic" gestures. But the symbolism is important, even central. For in this way Rush recognizes that the job of a Department of Peace is to change peoples' hearts and minds, and, as such, the job must start with the hearts and minds of the people who undertake the job. And it is something that cannot be done once and for all. On the contrary, it must be done day by day, one day at a time, unremittingly.

We must change the culture in which we live. That, as the cliché has it, is easier said than done. With climate change upon us, can we afford to waste so many resources and capacities on war? Dr. Benjamin Rush was not facing environmental catastrophe, and he had no knowledge of weapons with the power to devastate the earth's surface. But he saw the wisdom of peace.

Do we? Can we? Will we?

---

[7]   See Wikipedia: https://en.wikipedia.org/wiki/We_Are_the_World#USA_for_Africa_ musicians.

Why a Department of Peace?

Frederick L. Schuman

Design for War

More than 300 years ago, English philosopher Thomas Hobbes (1588–1679) wrote in his book on government and politics, *Leviathan* (1651), the following comment on international relations:

> In all times, kings, and persons of sovereign authority, because of their independency, are in continual jealousies, and in the state and posture of gladiators; having their weapons pointing, and their eyes fixed on one another; that is, their forts, garrisons and guns upon the frontiers of their kingdoms; and continual spies upon their neighbors; which is a posture of war.... The notions of right and wrong, justice and injustice, have there no place. Where there is no common power, there is no law: where no law, no injustice. Force and fraud are in war the two cardinal virtues.... It is consequent also to the same condition that there be no property, no dominion, no "mine" and "thine" distinct; but only that to be every man's that he can get; and for so long as he can keep it.

Hobbes was here calling attention to a simple fact of life pointed out by many predecessors, from Herodotus and Thucydides to Dante and Machiavelli and by many successors, yet long ignored by many seekers after peace—namely, that in any civilization in which political power is fragmented among separate sovereignties, the relations among the sovereignties are inevitably relations of rivalry in a competitive quest for security and therefore relations of potential or actual war.

Hence, every sovereign government has always maintained (and must maintain if it hopes to preserve its independence against enemies) military forces as heavily armed as it can afford. Hence, the need persists for general staffs, ministries or departments of war or defense, or comparable agencies, whatever they may be called, to direct those trained in the art of armed violence toward the protection and promotion of national purposes.

This ancient and honorable game of "power politics" is not a game which policy-makers of Great Powers are to play or not to play. Those who refuse to play lose the game. Those who condemn the game as evil, as undoubtedly it is in its usual consequences, are nevertheless obliged to play, as Americans have always done despite their moralistic disclaimers. Neither is the game a product of misunderstandings or divergent beliefs and values. When Francis I, was asked by a courtier: "What differences of views and interests, Your Majesty, cause you to constantly at war with your royal cousin, the Emperor Charles V?" The French monarch is said to have replied, "None at all. We are in perfect agreement. We both want control of Italy!" The point was more sharply put by the British economist R. G. Hawtrey in his *Economic Aspects of Sovereignty* (1930):

> When I say that the principle cause of war is war itself, I mean that the aim for which war is judged worthwhile is most often something which itself affects military power. Just as in military operations each side aims at getting

anything which will give it a military advantage, so in diplomacy each side aims at getting anything which will enhance its power. Diplomacy is potential war. It is permeated by the struggle for power and when potential breaks out into actual war, that is usually because irreconcilable claims have been made to some element of power, and neither side can claim such preponderance as to compel the other to give way by a mere threat.

The war system is thus self-perpetuating so long as sovereign states are rivals for power, as they must forever remain in a community of sovereignties lacking any higher authority to maintain and enforce peace, order, and law among its members.

Original Sin

The search for peace has long been dominated by common knowledge that all the founders of the world's higher religions have condemned violence. Renunciation of violence, it has long been argued, requires the moral reeducation of mankind and its rededication to ethical values. War is widely held to be implicit in human nature. This view, as we shall see, is false. But under certain circumstances it is true. In a symbolic sense at least, we are all alike victims of the first sin (disobedience) of Adam and Eve and, more miserably, of the second sin (murder) committed by Cain against Abel, his brother.

Let us be clear as to what is here involved lest we sink into further confusion. Recent studies of animal behavior (see Konrad Lorenz, *King Solomon's Ring*, 1952, and *On Aggression*, 1966, and Robert Ardrey, *The Territorial Imperative*, 1966) demonstrate that among vertebrate animals living in their natural habitats, only two

types ever kill other members of their own species: rats and men.[8]
No other beasts behave as "bestially" as human beings. Why this
is so is not our present concern. It is so.

On another level of motivation, Friedrich Wilhelm Nietzsche
(1844–1900), anticipating in his scattered aphorisms the later
findings of Sigmund Freud (1856–1939), observed:

> Say not that a good cause justifies any war. Say rather
> that a good war justifies any cause.... War affords the
> joys of cold-blooded murder with a good conscience....
> Whenever in our time a war breaks out, there also breaks
> out, and especially among the most noble members of the
> people, a secret desire. They throw themselves with delight
> against the new danger of death, because in the sacrifice
> for the fatherland they believe they have found at last the
> permission they have been seeking: the permission to evade
> their human purpose. War is for them a shortcut to suicide.
> It enables them to commit suicide with a good conscience.

Again, we need not here pursue these themes. Only a word of
warning is in order. Impulses, usually unconscious, toward murder
and suicide are constants of human nature and will long remain
so. Just so long, all efforts, assiduously pursued by searchers after
peace, to abolish war by dwelling upon its horrors, by praising the
glories of peace, and by urging friendship among nations will fail
of their purpose. Such efforts have gone on for many centuries,

---

[8]   Schuman's information is out of date. For a recent review of a wide variety of more
recent work in biology, anthropology, and history, see John Horgan, *The End of War* (San
Francisco: McSweeney's Books, 2012), and Douglas P. Frye, *The Human Potential for
Peace: An Anthropological Challenge to Assumptions about War and Violence* (New York:
Oxford University Press, 2006).

during which span of wars have become more frequent, more bloody, more destructive, more global, and more calculated, with the ever-accelerated tempo of science and technology, to enable mankind to commit mass murder and mass suicide with finality.

The Price of Peace

If war, as a pattern of human behavior as old as civilization, were in any direct sense a product of those aspects of human nature referred to above, then war would be as constant and continuous as civilization itself, with brief intervals for recovery from the last war and preparations for the next. This is not at all the case, as every student of history knows. At various times during the past 7,000 years of the human adventure, large populations inhabiting vast territories have lived in peace through many generations.[9]

Why and how? The answer is self-evident to anyone familiar with the record. In each such instance, the local sovereignties of rival communities were merged into a larger political entity whose rulers and people were able and willing to prevent recourse to force among the parts constituting a new whole. The case closest to us in space and time was, of course, the Roman Empire of ancient days. For all its crudities and cruelties, plus intermittent civil wars and conflicts with barbarians beyond the frontiers, the *Pax Romana* brought to Western mankind a larger and longer measure of peace, order, law, and justice than it ever knew before or has ever known since.

There was truth in the comment of the unknown writer (paralleled by comparable judgments by well-known contemporaries)

---

[9] For recent treatment of our capacity for peace, see Steven Pinker, *The Better Angels of Our Nature* (New York: Viking Books, 2011).

quoted by Edward Gibbon. The Romans, he wrote, celebrated "the increasing splendor the cities, the beautiful face of the country, cultivated and adorned like an immense garden; and the long festival of peace, which was enjoyed by so many nations, forgetful of their ancient animosities, and of apprehension of future danger."

Other examples come readily to mind. Such, briefly, was the case with the earlier empire of Alexander the Great. Such, much later, was the case with far-flung realms of the Saracens and of the Ottoman Turks. Such also was case with the most extensive and populous of all contiguous empires, extending from the Baltic to Burma and embracing perhaps two-thirds of the human race—namely, the Mongol Empire of the Khans, which kept the peace of most of Eurasia for many centuries. Some will see a counterpart in the widely scattered colonies and dominions of the *Pax Britannica* of more recent time. Always and invariably, peace was the result of the merging of separate and rival sovereignties into a vast imperium within which order and law, if not always justice, were maintained and enforced.

Dilemma

All thoughtful readers who have gotten thus far, before we have arrived at our central concern, will have noticed that all the "world states" or "universal empires" of times gone by were brought into being by the military subjugation of lesser states by the dominant "Superpower" of the epoch. This method of achieving world peace cannot be successfully employed in our time. Thanks to the politics of the "balance of power," all such efforts, whether by Hapsburgs or Bourbons or Bonaparts or Hohenzollerns or Lenins or Stalins or Hitlers or Hirohitos, have always ended in disastrous failure, usually in the wake of colossal expenditures of blood and treasure by those determined to thwart and cast down each successive aspirant to world domination.

There has been no exception to this rule for the past five centuries. There is no reason to suppose that there will be any exceptions for the next five centuries—if our civilization and our species may dare to hope for so long a future. Those who seek to achieve world order and world peace by military conquest or revolution or propaganda for purpose of arriving at a global *Pax Americana* or *Pax Sovietica* or *Pax Sinica* are victims of a tragic delusion. World War III, if we permit it to come, will not eventuate in one Rome, but in two or many Carthages. Why this is inevitable has been sufficiently spelled out in the literature of our time to need no further elaboration here.

Do we have available any alternative route toward world order and world peace? In theory, but not as yet in practice, we do. The alternative is voluntary and cooperative agreement among the now multitudinous sovereignties of our state system, 140 at latest count,[10] to insure survival and avoid extinction by establishing some semblance of world government above and beyond the nation-states. Such was the hope of Woodrow Wilson. The effort failed by virtue of fear (not only in America but elsewhere) that the League of Nations would somehow infringe on the sacred sovereignty of the member states. Such was the hope of the founders of the United Nations. The enterprise, albeit useful and hopeful, has for the same reason not yet proven a success. Such is the hope of contemporary federalists, who contend, on the basis of past experience, that the classical theory of collective security (i.e., peace-keeping through

---

[10]   The United Nations had 193 member states as of 2008. Depending on how you count them, the world may contain three more nation-states.

coercion of states by states) is unworkable and that the alternative road requires a limited area of world law enforced on individuals on the local level as in true federation, including the United States of America.

For this new departure on a world scale, or even on a regional scale, humanity today is obviously not yet ready. Therefore, other and more limited approaches to the most fateful, and possibly fatal, problem of our time are in order.

A Modest Proposal

Among these approaches is a relatively simple one. It is not new, as we shall see. It has been proposed many times by many thoughtful citizens and law-makers. It is not a panacea. There are no panaceas for the disorders of our civilization. But it offers opportunities for new thinking and for valuable contributions to the common cause.

The proposal is that there be established a Department of Peace under a Secretary of Peace in the federal cabinet of the USA—and, if possible, in other governments—charged with the unique responsibility of searching out ways of resolving by nonviolent means the inevitable conflicts of interests, expectations, and ambitions among national sovereignties and advising the Chief Executive, as other ministries or departments advise him or her in their respective spheres, as to the most effective procedures for avoiding war and promoting peace. All of this, it is hoped, will be in anticipation of successive international "crises," which will always be with us, rather than in hurried responses to unforeseen conflicts. Such responses have often proved too little and too late to avoid calamitous mistakes in policy-making.

Senator Alexander Wiley of Wisconsin, speaking in the Senate, June 27, 1945, on the new UN charter, declared: "Mr. President, on July 7, 1943, I spoke on the floor of the Senate in relation to a Department of Peace. I stated at that time that I craved for my Government the distinction of being the first Government on earth to establish a Secretary of Peace. The establishment of such a secretariat would be heralded throughout the world." As of 1968–1969: not yet.

The simplicity and logic of the proposal are so persuasive that most of us who have not looked into the matter will be astonished at the complexities allegedly involved and at the curious history of frustration thus marking the enterprise. Let us try, at the risk of oversimplification and inevitable omissions, to review the record. Boredom can be avoided by bearing in mind the central purpose of the proposal amid variations of detail.

It is also well to bear in mind that during the days of our years there is no novelty in the establishment of new executive departments in Washington. The Department of Health, Education, and Welfare was created by Act of Congress, April 11, 1953; the Department of Housing and Urban Development by Act of Congress, September 9, 1965; and the Department of Transportation by Act of Congress, October 15, 1966.[11] Each of these has performed necessary and highly useful functions, as would also be the case with a Department of Peace.

Old Wine in New Bottles

The new republic was confronted with numerous embarrass-

---

[11] What about changes since this pamphlet was written, for example, the Department of Homeland Security?

ments, vexations, and conflicts in its foreign relations during the first decade of the Federal Constitution, 1789–1799. Apart from Indian wars, the French Revolution confronted President Washington's administration with grave issues. A general European war began in 1792. The United States was allied with France by the Treaty of February 6, 1778. Pro-British and pro-French factions in Congress, the press, and the public quarreled bitterly. In 1793 the new administration chose a course of neutrality, but granted recognition to the revolutionary regime in Paris by receiving Citizen Genet as French Minister. Both belligerents in their efforts to blockade one another seized American ships and seamen. A fresh conflict with England was barely avoided by the controversial and unpopular Jay Treaty of 1794. Two years later, in his Farewell Address, President Washington warned against foreign entanglements. In 1798 Congress abrogated the French treaties. Among the results was an undeclared naval war with France at the close of the decade.

Under these perilous circumstances, many concerned Americans sought new departures from prevailing procedures for policy-making. Among them was a proposal for an Office or Department of Peace. Its original authorship is still controversial, but two distinguished Americans of the 1790s, one black and one white, share honors. In the fall of 1792 appeared in Philadelphia the first edition of Banneker's *Almanack and Ephemeris for the Year of our Lord 1793*. It contained an essay, which began as follows:

> Among the defects which have been pointed out in the Federal Constitution by its antifederal enemies, it is much to be lamented that no person has taken notice of its total silence upon the subject of an *office* of the utmost importance to the welfare of the United States, that is,

an office for promoting and preserving perpetual peace in our country.

It is to be hoped that no objection will be made in the establishment of such an office, while we are engaged in a war with the Indians, for as the *War-Office* of the United States was established in the time of peace, it is equally reasonable that a *Peace-Office* should be established in the time of *war*....

Let a Secretary of the Peace be appointed to preside in this office, who shall be perfectly free from all the present absurd and vulgar European prejudices upon the subject of government; let him be a genuine republican and sincere Christian, for the principles of republicanism and Christianity are no less friendly to universal and perpetual peace than they are to universal and equal liberty.

The editor was Benjamin Banneker (1731–1806), sometimes called the "black Ben Franklin"—a freeborn Maryland Negro who continued his *Almanack* for a decade and won wide recognition in the USA and in Europe as surveyor, mathematician, and astronomer. The unsigned article may have been his own or may have been the anonymous contribution of his friend, Dr. Benjamin Rush (1745–1813), a physician, pamphleteer, social reformer, medical educator, and signer of the Declaration of Independence. In 1799 the good Dr. Rush wrote "A Plan of a Peace-Office for the United States," identical in language (save for an addenda on the horrors of war) with the essay of 1792. Curiously enough, the "Plan" never appeared in print until 1947, but no doubt was discussed in the

1790s by Banneker, Rush, Jefferson, and others in conversations forever lost to us.

The honor of priority, if ever ascertainable, is best left to researchers in old archives. It is enough to observe that the project of a Department of Peace first emerged in the 1790s with its author or authors regarding the Department primarily as an educational and hortatory agency designed to convince Americans of the virtue of peace and the criminality of war.

The proposal was later echoed during the course of the 19th Century by various publicists and legislators. Since their efforts were without result, we need not here review them except to note that the idea of a Department of Peace continued at intervals to attract the attention of those given to thoughtful reflection. The far more numerous proposals of the twentieth century deserve closer study if only because there is a chance, despite many past discouragements, that they may lead to constructive action.

Note: From this point forward in these pages, all dates in parentheses, unless otherwise indicated, refer to the *Congressional Record*, where those wishing to pursue the problem further will find all relevant speeches, bills, documents, quotations, citations, and other material bearing upon the issue.

A Surfeit of Projects

In the 74th, 75th, and 76th Congresses, Senator Matthew Neely of West Virginia repeatedly presented his bill (1935, 1937, 1939) to establish a department of peace. World War II diminished congressional interest in such proposals, but it enhanced the hopes of those who saw merit in the idea. As already noted, Senator Alexander Wiley of Wisconsin revived the plan in the midst of war (July 7, 1943) and several times subsequently. Immediately after V-E Day, Senator Karl Mundt of North Dakota addressed his colleagues: "Needed: A Department of Peace" (May 10, 1945). Representative Louis Ludlow of Indiana introduced and explained another bill (November 12, 1945) and spoke (December 21, 1945) on "Why we should have a Department of Peace." Representative (later Senator) Everett Dirksen of Illinois introduced a bill for "A Peace Division in the State Department" (H. J. Res. 13, January 3, 1947).

Following a hiatus of several years, Senator Hubert H. Humphrey of Minnesota introduced S. 2987 to establish a National Peace Agency (February 4, 1960). Between the 84th Congress and the 90th Congress, 1955–1968, no less than eighty-five bills were introduced in the House or Senate to create a Department of Peace. At the time of writing, the most recent of these (see below) were introduced by Representative Seymour Halpern of New York and Senator Vance Hartke of Indiana (September 10, 1968, and September 11, 1968).

Not all of these bills, to be sure, were proposals de novo. Some were duplicates of others, and some were the same bills reintroduced at successive sessions. Nevertheless, their number and variety render any comparison impossible in brief compass. Nor is this needful for present purposes. The Legislative Reference Service of the Library of Congress has prepared summaries and analyses of some of the bills—for example, *Analysis of H.R. 4005, 81st Congress, to establish a Department of Peace* (Hugh L. Elsbree, May 13, 1949); *Analysis of H.R. 3190, A Bill to Create a National Peace Agency* (Margaret Fennell, February 24, 1961); same (Louis C. Woolf, April 25, 1961); *The Historical Development of Past Legislation to Establish a*

U.S. Department of Peace, with Reasons and Statements in Support of the Proposal: Report Prepared According to the Instructions of the Hon. Spark Matsunaga, Hawaii (Ernest S. Lent, October 22, 1968).

Whose Cause?

What is striking in these legislative proposals, apart from their multiplicity and their general conformity to common purposes, is the wide range of approval they have received. There is no issue here between Democrats and Republicans, between labor and business, between "liberals" and "conservatives," among Catholics, Protestants, and Jews, or among racial groups or sections of the country.

A study of the *Congressional Record* and of the daily and periodical press will reveal, to select a few examples, support for a Department of Peace by Kirby Page in a pamphlet published in the mid-1920s by the Council of Christian Associations (YMCA and YWCA); several locals of the United Mine Workers of America; such otherwise divergent columnists as Drew Pearson and David Lawrence; publisher Frank E. Gannett to President-elect Eisenhower (letter of January 13, 1953); *The Bulletin of the Atomic Scientists,* February and September, 1960; the Democratic Advisory Council in a statement of December 5, 1959; Trevor Gardner, former Assistant Secretary of the Air Force; *ACT,* publication of the Catholic Christian Family Movement (October issue, 1968); the *Milwaukee Catholic Herald Citizen,* November 1, 1968; James G. Patton, President of the United World Federalists (October 9, 1968); Norman Cousins, President of the World Association of World Federalists (October 9, 1968); *The Baptist Press*; Women's International League for Peace and Freedom; Women's Strike for Peace; Friends Committee on National Legislation; and Another Mother for Peace; etc.

I can find no record, thus far, of any organized or articulate opposition, either inside or outside the halls of Congress, to a projected Department of Peace.

The Inertia of Inaction

Given the record already reviewed, most participant observers of the democratic process must be mystified by the absence, to date, of any progress toward the goal. None of the bills has thus far been debated or voted upon in either the Senate or the House. None has ever been reported out of committee. Hearings have been held in only a few instances: on H.R. 3628, a Bill to Create a Department of Peace (introduced by Representative Jennings Randolph), Committee on Foreign Affairs, House of Representatives, 79th Congress, 1st session (November 8, 1945); same on Senator Wiley's bill, with House counterparts introduced by Representatives Randolph and Louis Ludlow; and Hearings in House Committee on Expenditures of the Executive Department (June 18, 1947), To Create a Department of Peace—Senator Wiley's Bill again supported by Senator Chapman Revercomb and Representatives Melvin Snyder and Everett Dirksen. Since 1947: no hearings, no reports, no debates, and no votes.

Why? The simplest answer, and perhaps the best, is that there has not yet emerged a sufficiently widespread and insistent public demand for a Department of Peace to move Congress to legislative action—to say nothing of the Executive Branch, which, up to now, has taken no initiative in the matter. On another and less obvious plane of purposes, let it be noted that all proposals for peace, including the present one, are deemed commendable in every nation of patriots, providing that nothing is done *to* give them concrete meaning. With few exceptions, such projects make no enemies, win some friends, and have no immediately visible or tangible effects on the distribution of wealth and income.

Conversely, appropriations for "defense" and even for the waging of war, particularly if they are of the magnitude prevailing in America in recent years, win widespread patriotic support and spell jobs, wages, salaries, and profits to important interest groups in the context of the military-industrial complex, against which President Eisenhower sternly warned, in vain, in his Farewell Address of January 17, 1961. To oppose the voting of money or the enactment of laws for such purposes is to invite charges of lack of patriotism, "letting the boys down," unconcern for "national security," and even "disloyalty." Few candidates for election or reelection to Congress can afford to take such risks. Thus, for example, the Gulf of Tonkin Resolution of 1964, which became the basis for the Johnson administration's waging of a massive and vastly expensive undeclared war in Vietnam, was passed unanimously in the House, August 7, and was opposed by only two senators out of a hundred. Although the ensuing war was by far the most unpopular ever waged by the USA, both senators voting against it (Morse and Gruening) were defeated in 1968.

We are here in the presence of a paradox which is world-wide. Sir Norman Angell in a famous book, *The Great Illusion*—first published in 1910, translated into twenty languages, read by millions of people, and republished in amplified form in 1933—demonstrated beyond doubt that under twentieth-century conditions war does not "pay"; that "military power is socially and economically futile; that it is impossible for one nation to seize by force the wealth or trade of another"; and that "war, even when victorious, can no longer achieve those aims for which people strive."

Sir Norman was, quite rightly, later knighted and awarded the Nobel Peace Prize. What he ignored or minimized was this: all wars, despite temporary illusions to the contrary, are ultimately ruinous to the wealth and welfare of all the participants. But each war, with popular patriotic support, is hugely lucrative in honors or money or both to the war-makers, to the arms-makers, and to their executives, stockholders, and employees. An effective Department of Peace might conceivably interfere with this pleasant and profitable process—which, if persisted in, is a primrose path to perdition.

Here, once more, we need not pursue our current theme. Let two quotations suffice. The always sardonic Thorstein B. Veblen (1857–1929) wrote in his *Inquiry Into the Nature of Peace* (1919):

Any politician who succeeds in embroiling his country in a war, however nefarious, becomes a popular hero and is reputed a wise and righteous statesman, at least for the time being. Illustrative instances need perhaps not, and indeed cannot gracefully, be named; most popular heroes and reputed statesmen belong in this class.... Since the ethical values involved in any given international contest are substantially of the nature of after-thought or accessory, they may safely be left on one side in any endeavor to understand or account for any given outbreak of hostilities. The moral indignation of both parties to the quarrel is to be taken for granted, as being the statesman's chief and necessary ways and means of bringing any war-like enterprise to a head and floating it to a creditable finish. It is a precipitate of the partisan animosity that inspires both parties and holds them to their duty of self-sacrifice and devastation, and at its best will chiefly serve as a cloak of self-righteousness to extenuate any exceptionally profligate excursions in the conduct of hostilities.

More succinctly, Edith Cavell (1865–1915), the British Army nurse in occupied Belgium during World War I who was court-martialed for aiding the escape of British prisoners, is reported to have said shortly before her execution by a German firing squad: "Patriotism is not enough."

Why Not the Department of State?

Among Americans who have given thought to the problem, some have concluded that the projected functions of a Department of Peace are performed, or ought to be performed, by the venerable Department of State. This is a misconception of governmental responsibility. The contention is plausible on the premise that problems of power in world politics can be resolved only by war or by diplomacy. Since the Department of State and the Foreign Service are charged with the conduct of diplomacy, their purpose might seem to some to be the promotion of peace. This is not the case, has never been the case, and cannot ever be the case in the nature of things.

The considerations to be adduced in support of this view have nothing to do with the long-standing and ever-mounting criticisms of the State Department. We are here confronted with a public bureaucracy that, like all others, proliferates at an ever-increasing pace. The department had 8 employees in Washington in 1790, 52 in 1870, 209 in 1909, 631 in 1922, 963 in 1938, 2,750 in 1943, and 23,000 in 1957, including 16,500 in foreign posts. By 1966 the department employed 43,000 people, 30,000 of them abroad, and was costing the taxpayers almost half a billion dollars a year—a miniscule sum, to be sure, compared to the Pentagon. Some critics contended that this bureaucracy had, willy-nilly, become a mere adjunct of the Pentagon, the Joint Chiefs of Staff, and the Central Intelligence Agency and no longer played a meaningful role in the formulation of foreign policy. In the unkindest cut of all against "Foggy Bottom," President Kennedy once said that the Department was "a bowl of jelly.... They never have any ideas over there, never come up with anything new."

Regardless of the truth or falsity of such allegations, the central point is simple: the function of the State Department and Foreign Service is neither to foster peace nor prevent war, but to promote the "national interests" of the USA as defined by the President, the Secretary of State, and their colleagues and collaborators. Any deviation from this duty reduces to futility the entire diplomatic bureaucracy. The duty itself has nothing to do, per se, with peace or war. To paraphrase the classic dictum of Carl von Clausewitz ("War is politics continued by other means"), diplomacy is war continued by other means—namely, a quest for national advantage in competition with rivals and potential or actual enemies.

The point was well put by John Foster Dulles before a House Appropriations Subcommittee, June 18, 1957:

> Not for one minute do I think the purpose of the State Department is to make friends. The purpose of the State Department is to look out for the interests of the United States. Whether we make friends I do not care.... We try to maintain friendly relations with some foreign countries, not all.... If the making of these loans saves a country from Communism, I do not care whether they like us or hate us. We will have accomplished our purpose....

[What follows] will be a problem for some other Secretary of State, not me.

With the wisdom of hindsight, some might question the desirability or possibility of "saving the world from Communism." No sensible critic can question the Secretary's insistence that the State Department exists to serve the national interest.

The Department of State has long been plagued with functions having little relation to the conduct of foreign affairs. In 1829, when the Department was charged with the census, coinage, territorial records, patents, and copyrights, Andrew Jackson commented: "I am impressed with the importance of so organizing the Department that its Secretary may devote more of his time to our foreign relations." Numerous reorganizations have since ensued. The problem remains, but is not our present concern.

Civil servants, including diplomats, resemble all other human beings in fearing change lest change should jeopardize tenures and careers. In the present case, such fears are unfounded. Whatever agencies of the State Department may be transferred to the Department of Peace (see below) would retain the existing personnel with a possibly more hopeful prospect of imaginative and creative contributions. Such transfers might indeed promote the economy and efficiency of the Foreign Service. Professional and veteran diplomat Ellis O. Briggs, in *The National Observer*, June 17, 1963, records reminiscence worth quoting:

> Many of our diplomatic missions could perform twice as effectively with half the personnel now infesting the premises.... Fourteen years ago, in Czechoslovakia, the State Department instructed me to survey Prague staffing

needs, following the Communist seizure of the country, at which time the American staff numbered 80. Six months after my recommendation, approved by the State Department, that personnel be reduced to 40, I had managed to get rid of *two* persons—only two—and one of them was transferred from Prague and not replaced, a device which I seem to recall is referred to in the world of bureaucracy as attrition. Today, a decade and a half later, it exhausts me to remember the struggle with Washington to obtain that reduction from 80 to 78 persons. If I had started to dig the projected Nicaraguan canal with a teaspoon, those six months might have shown more impressive achievement....

It was at that point that the Communists got into the act. Far as I know, they had no idea of the personnel war I was fighting—and losing—with Washington. They possibly thought they were dealing the American ambassador the most painful blow imaginable when they suddenly declared five-sixths of my staff *persona non grata.* They gave the embassy two weeks to get 66 American employees and all their families over the border.

For 30 months thereafter I ran the American embassy in Prague with 12 individuals—13 counting the ambassador.... It was the most efficient embassy I ever had.... The State Department, after it recovered from the shock, declared it was delighted with the embassy's performance....

Another clarification about supernumeraries is relevant.

They are not, in the main, State Department supernumeraries.... During World War II the State Department and its overseas personnel were rather generally pushed aside, and the military took over diplomacy. Since the surrender of Germany and Japan brought no peace but the Cold War, the military remain today very much—and very willingly—in the diplomatic picture. At my last post I discovered on arrival that my Pentagon attaché complement numbered over 70 officers and enlisted men. Seventy American soldiers, sailors, and airman, all attached to one embassy. Had I been able to deploy them for three hours every morning in full dress uniforms, playing leapfrog across the Acropolis, that would have made as much sense as most of the duties they solemnly declared they were engaged in....

The prospective relations between a Department of Peace and the Department of State cannot be plotted in advance. Their functions would be quite different for reasons already indicated. Should frictions develop between them, the result might be helpful rather than hurtful. As Senator Jennings Randolph put it (July 2, 1959): "It would not be the first instance of interdepartmental conflict in our Government.... Such a possibility might be an argument favoring the creation of a Department of Peace ... forcing the State Department, as it were, to defend its positions."

Why Not the United Nations?

The framers of the United Nations Charter at San Francisco in the spring of 1945 were more realistic than the framers of the League of Nations Covenant in Paris in the spring of 1919. They took it for granted that the new league could function effectively as a vehicle of world peace only on the basis of a "Concert of Power" among the Great Powers of the world. They therefore provided, in accordance with the "Yalta Formula" agreed upon in February 1945, by Roosevelt, Churchill, and Stalin in the Crimea, that (Art. 27) "decisions of the Security Council" in all substantive matters (e.g., so-called "peace enforcement action") "shall be made by an affirmative vote of seven members including the concurring votes of the permanent members"—that is, the USA, the USSR, Britain, France, and China. This "veto" article was, and still is, widely misunderstood. It meant, quite clearly, that the framers of the Charter were aware that any coercion of states by states in accordance with the classic doctrine of collective security, now widely regarded as unworkable under most circumstances, would require the unanimity of the Great Powers in order to be effective.

The alternative to the "veto," which was an American, not a Soviet, proposal, would have been the prospect of one or another or several of the major states using economic or military coercion against another major state, or one of its allies, without the consent of, and in the face of the opposition of, the Great Power resisting coercion. The only possible result would be not world peace but another world war. Only those who have not thought through the issue would place their hopes in what Charles A. Beard once ridiculed as "perpetual war for perpetual peace."

This inevitable limitation on the political efficacy of the United Nations would have been of no consequence if, as the framers of the Charter hoped and assumed, the wartime concert of the Great Powers had continued in the sense of a minimum common accord on common interests. The hope waned with the advent of Cold War in 1945-46 and vanished in the Chinese Revolution of 1949.

Responsibility for the result, assumed by most Americans to reside in "Communist" ambitions of world domination and by most Russians and Chinese to reside in "capitalist" ambitions of world domination, is not our present problem. What is important for all people to realize is that under these conditions the United Nations cannot "keep the peace," as events have abundantly demonstrated through a quarter of a century.

As for the General Assembly as the "town meeting of the world," its usefulness is obvious, despite much nonsense spoken at its sessions. Here again many misconceptions remain to be resolved. One of them, perhaps the major one, was well put by Dr. Brock Chisholm, the distinguished Canadian psychiatrist, once director of the World Health Organization and of the World Association for Mental Health. In his book, *Prescription for Survival* (1957), Dr. Chisholm wrote:

> Very frequently one hears the United Nations criticized as a debating society. That's primarily what it is for. It is there to provide an opportunity for governments to talk out the world's problems. Many people might accept the idea of the debating society, but interpret it to mean that the United Nations is a place where we go to reproach other people for being the way they are. This is an old, old habit. Man's method of dealing with difficulty in the past has always been to tell everyone else how they should behave. We've all been doing that for centuries. It should be clear by now that this no longer does any good. Everybody has by now been told by everybody else how he should behave. Therefore, everybody knows how everybody else thinks he should behave. The criticism is

not effective; it never has been and it is never going to be. There is only one telling that is effective—our telling ourselves how to behave.

The United Nations is ill-adapted to promote the purpose which Dr. Chisholm rightly deems essential. Yet here is a vast fabric of functional international organizations devoted to the service of universal human needs: the Economic and Social Council; the Educational, Scientific and Cultural Organization (UNESCO); the Food and Agricultural Organization; the International Bank for Reconstruction and Development; the International Monetary Fund; the International Civil Aviation Organization; the International Labor Organization; the World Health Organization; the United Nations International Children's Emergency Fund (UNICEF); the Universal Postal Union; and a large number of other international unions affiliated with the UN in one way or another.

Much can be said in favor of making a Department of Peace the liaison agency between the USA and all of the *multilateral* international organizations, leaving to the State Department and the Foreign Service the conduct of *bilateral* negotiations with other governments. A further possibility deserves exploration. Thus far, with frequently unhappy results, spokesmen for the USA on the Security Council and in the General Assembly have been named by, and have been answerable to, the Secretary of State in the name of the President. At the very outset, before the UN had come formally into being, Senator Wiley (July 6, 1945) suggested that "the head of this Department, the Secretary of Peace, would be ex officio the delegate of the United States on the United Nations Security Council." In any case it would seem desirable that US representatives on the Council and in the Assembly should be appointed by, and responsible to, the Chief Executive by way of, and on the advice of, the proposed Secretary of Peace.

Here and Now

The 1968 proposal for a Department of Peace, as presented to the 2nd Session of the 90th Congress, was H.R. 19650, presented by Representative Seymour Halpern of New York with thirty cosponsors in the House, and paralleled by S. 4019, introduced by Senators Hartke, Hatfield, Yarborough, and Randolph.

For those allergic to legislative language, a resume may be helpful. These bills contemplate a Department of Peace to be headed by a Secretary of Peace; and an Undersecretary of Peace, four Assistant Secretaries of Peace, and a General Counsel, all to be appointed by the President and confirmed by the Senate. To the new Department shall be transferred from the Department of State the Agency for International Development, the Peace Corps, and the Arms Control and Disarmament Agency; from the Department of Agriculture, the International Agricultural Development Service; from the Department of Commerce, the Bureau of International Commerce as related to the General Agreement on Tariffs and Trade; the Export-Import Bank of the United States; and from other departments and agencies such functions as the President may determine on the advice of the Director of the Bureau of the Budget. Provisions for financing, personnel, administration annual report, research, publications, and litigation are comparable to those already in effect for other executive departments and agencies.

The Department is to establish an International Peace Institute to train citizens for public service. Its Board of Trustees is to consist of the Secretary and two assistants, two senators, two representatives, one member of the Atomic Energy Commission, one member of the Federal Council on the Arts and the Humanities, one member of the National Academy of Sciences, and two educators. The Institute is to be a one-year coeducational graduate school, limited to 150 students selected on the basis of competitive examinations, with each student obligated, upon completion of the program, to one year of public service in the cause of peace.

In its 1968 version, the bill also provides for a "Peace by Investment Corporation," initially as a public agency and ultimately under private ownership and management. Finally, the bill envisages in Congress a Joint Committee on Peace, to be composed of seven senators and seven representatives for study of, and recommendations regarding, problems of peace and the activities of the Department.

The 1969 version of the proposal took the form of a revised House bill, H.R. 6501, offered by Representative Halpern on February 6, cosponsored by sixty-two colleagues in the House (referred to the Committee on Government Operations), and an identical bill, S. 953, offered by Senator Hartke on February 7, cosponsored by fourteen colleagues in the upper chamber and referred to the Committee on Foreign Relations.

The revised bill, reflecting careful study and constructive thought and pending at the time of writing before the 1st Session of the 91st Congress (February 6 and 7, 1969), is, as compared with its precursor, briefer, clearer, and more explicit in its statement of objectives and more acceptable to more Congressmen and citizens. The general structure and purposes of the Department are as outlined above. The transfer of functions to the new Department, with minor modifications, are as previously contemplated—with, however, the relation of the Export-Import Bank and the projected "Peace by Investment Corporation" left open, no doubt wisely, pending further analysis of the problems involved. "The Secretary of Peace shall advise the President with respect to the appointment of any person to represent the United States in the United Nations, or in any of its organs, commissions, specialized agencies, or other bodies." Fully retained are the promising projects of an "International Peace Institute" and of a congressional body, now renamed the "Joint Congressional Committee on Peace and International Cooperation."

In the light of current and future discussions of the issues here posed, it may be useful to emphasize anew that a Department of Peace would in no way infringe upon, or "downgrade," the Department of State and the Foreign Service in the exercise of their proper and necessary functions—namely, the conduct of the bilateral diplomatic relations of the republic, the protection of citizens abroad, and the promotion of the national interest, none of which has any direct relevance to planning for peace.

Planning for war has been a major preoccupation of all national governments for many centuries. No useful purpose is served by pretending that planning for war fosters peace. The contrary has long been the case. People get what they plan for, not the opposite, whatever semantic obfuscations they choose to entertain, including the familiar slogan: Our war aim is peace. Just as the Department of State has its necessary functions to perform, so the Department of Defense has its equally necessary functions to perform. Many among us, dedicated to "preparedness," "deterrence," "containment," and comparable objectives, essential as they often are, are still bewitched, albeit unknowingly, by the ancient Roman adage: *si vis pacem, para bellum*—if you wish peace, prepare for war.

For reasons already here suggested, this injunction has no applicability in the world in which we live. It had validity in the Rome of old only because the long invincible Roman Legions, directed by Consuls and Emperors who often seemed to be building a World Empire in fits of absence of mind, ultimately extinguished the political independence of all of Rome's neighbors and rivals and thus put an end to power politics in the ancient state system of the West. This is now an impossibility, even for the most formidable of "Superpowers." The Departments of State and Defense must carry on their necessary tasks. They deserve to be supplemented by a Department of Peace.

Promise and Prospect

In view of the illusions that have bedeviled "peace movements" throughout the world for many generations, no one can reasonably assume that a federal Department of Peace in Washington will solve the problem. The unavoidable limitations of its activities have been suggested in the opening pages of this chapter. Nonetheless, the establishment of a Department of Peace would not only constitute the contemporary realization of an ideal almost as old as the Republic, but would open out opportunities for rethinking and restudying of old issues and for a new area of creative public service of incalculable value. The cause of human welfare and human survival can never be insured by mechanical rearrangements of governmental machinery. But such rearrangements can contribute and have often in the past contributed, to a reorientation of attitudes and activities in a constructive direction. In our own time of troubles, as in an earlier one, it is not sentimentalism or romanticism but simple realism to recall words of Abraham Lincoln in 1862:

In times like the present, men should utter nothing for which they would not willingly be responsible through time and in eternity.... The dogmas of the quiet past are inadequate to the stormy present. The occasion is piled high with difficulty, and we must rise with the occasion. As our case is new, so we must think anew and act anew. We must disenthrall ourselves.... Fellow-citizens, we cannot escape history.... No personal significance or insignificance can spare one or another of us. The fiery trail through which we pass will light us down, in honor or dishonor, to the latest generation. We shall nobly save or meanly lose the last best hope of earth.

At a time when senators and representatives increasingly feel that their constitutional role in foreign affairs has been ignored by the Executive, the Congressional Joint Committee on Peace could inaugurate a new era, at once in harmony with American political traditions and conducive to a new pattern of foreign policy directed toward the nonviolent resolution of international controversies. At a time when the hazardous gap between rich and poor nations is ever widening, some form of a "Peace by Investment Corporation" might play a significant role in narrowing the breach. At a time when many young people feel alienated from the absurdity, injustice, and violence of a world they never made, an International Peace Institute could inspire a new dedication to creative action. At a time when US foreign policy has reached an all-time low in futility and frustration, a Department of Peace could initiate a new and more hopeful era.

No one can guarantee any such results. But to ignore the opportunity implicit in a new enterprise would be a betrayal of the meaning of America and a gesture of despair over the possibility of peace among nations.

Given the long record of the past, it must by now be clear that a Department of Peace will come into being only if an overwhelming majority of American citizens of all parties, all creeds, all classes, all races, and all sections make abundantly clear to their elective spokesmen in Washington that they are resolved that this new departure should be undertaken. Without such a public demand, nothing can be accomplished. With it, much is possible. Seldom have the citizens of the Republic been summoned to support a more worthy and hopeful cause.

Cosponsors of S. 953 and H.R. 6501 in the 91st Congress

When this pamphlet was originally published, two bills, S. 953 in the Senate and H.R. 6501 in the House of Representatives, were before the 91st Congress. They are identical.

Cosponsors of S. 953, introduced in the Senate by Senator Vance Hartke (D-IN):

Birch Bayh (D-IN.)   Edmund S. Muskie (D-ME)
Robert C. Byrd (D-WV)   Gaylord Nelson (D-WI)
Alan Cranston (D-CA)   Claiborne Pell (D-RI)
Mark O. Hatfield (R-OR)   Jennings Randolph (D-WV)
Daniel K. Inouye (D-HI)   Abraham A. Ribicoff (D-CT)
Mike Mansfield (D-MO)   Ralph W. Yarborough (D-TX)
Lee Matcalf (D-MO)   Stephen M. Young (D-OH)

Cosponsors of H.R. 6501, introduced in the House of Representatives by Congressman Seymour Halpern (R-NY):

Joseph P. Addabbo (D-NY)   Alphonzo Bell (R-CA)

Mario Biaggi (D-NY)
John A. Blatnik (D-MN)
Edward P. Boland (D-MA)
Frank J. Brasco (D-NY)
George E. Brown, Jr. (D-CA)
Phillip Burton (D-CA)
Daniel E. Button (R-NY)
James A. Byrne (D-PA)
Shirley Chisholm (D-NY)
Silvio O. Conte (R-MA)
John Conyers, Jr. (D-MI)
Glenn Cunningham (R-NE)
Dominick V. Daniels (D-NJ)
John R. Dellenback (R-OR)
John H. Dent (D-PA)
Charles C. Diggs, Jr. (D-MI)
Harold D. Donohue (D-MA)
Thaddeus J. Dulski (D-NY)
Florence P. Dwyer (R-NY)
Don Edwards (D-CA)
Joshua Eilberg (D-PA)
Leonard Farbstein (D-NY)
Donald M. Fraser (D-MN)
Samuel N. Friedel (D-MD)
James G. Fulton (R-PA)
Richard H. Fulton (D-TN)
Jacob Gilbert (D-NY)
Kenneth J. Gray (D-IL)
Augustus F. Hawkins (D-CA)
Margaret M. Heckler (R-MA)
Henry Helstoski (D-NJ)
Frank Horton (R-NY)
Andrew Jacobs, Jr. (D-IN)
Charles S. Joelson (D-NJ)

Joseph E. Karth (D-MN)
Edward I. Koch (D-NY)
Clarence D. Long (D-MD)
Paul N. McCloskey, Jr. (R-CA)
Spark M. Matsunaga (D-HI)
Abner J. Mikva (D-IL)
Joseph G. Minish (D-NJ)
Robert H. Mollohan (D-WV)
William S. Moorhead (D-PA)
Robert N. C. Nix (D-PA)
Arnold Olsen (D-MO)
Richard L. Ottinger (D-NY)
Thomas M. Pelly (R-WA)
Claude Pepper (D-FL)
Bertram L. Podell (D-NY)
Thomas M. Rees (D-CA)
Henry S. Reuss (D-WI)
Benjamin S. Rosenthal (D-NY)
Edward R. Roybal (D-CA)
William F. Ryan (D-NY)
William L. St. Onge (D-CT)
James H. Scheuer (D-NY)
Harley O. Staggers (D-WV)
Leonor K. Sullivan (D-MO)
Charles A. Vanik (D-OH)
Jerome R. Waldie (D-CA)
Charles H. Wilson (D-CA)

Peace Is Everybody's Business; Nobody's Job

Mary Liebman and Bill Benzon

From Rush to the 91st Congress

In 1966 Mary Liebman read Benjamin Rush's 1793 proposal for a Peace-Office in the United States. It made sense. "A peace office might help modern man beat the Last Neanderthal to the switch," she wrote in one of the newsletters she wrote in the 1970s as part of a considerable effort to have a department of peace established in the federal government.

When she and her colleagues began working, they didn't know that the idea had been brought before Congress several times earlier in the century nor that other groups had begun mobilizing support for a department of peace. But they soon found out:

> The most vigorous effort was directed by a California-based organization, Another Mother for Peace, which in February 1969, brought a large number of well-trained citizen-lobbyists including many Hollywood celebrities, to the Capitol to dramatize the presentation of bills by Senator Vance Hartke and Representative Seymour Halpern. Shortly thereafter, at the suggestion of the sponsors, a Peace Act Advisory Council was formed, to coordinate the activities of groups favoring the bills. Peace people, political scientists and other academicians, and representatives of every religious denomination joined

the Council, but as it turned out, the volunteers of the peace brigade had their hands full fighting their own fires [remember, this was the height of the Vietnam War]; campus concern took a totally different direction; and a year later it was still possible for a clergyman in Minnesota to publish an article in *The Churchman*, calling for a Department of Peace in the Cabinet without either author or editor knowing of the existence of the Hartke-Halpern bills.[12]

On February 7, 1969, Senator Vance Hartke (D-IN) and Representative Seymour Halpern (R-NY) had introduced bills into the 91st Congress to create a US Department of Peace—S. 953 in the Senate with fourteen sponsors and H.R. 6501 in the House with sixty-seven sponsors, respectively. The Peace Act Advisory Council (PAAC) met for the first time in November of that year:

> Most members were nominated by voluntary organizations working in programs related to peace, international cooperation, and foreign affairs. The Council is not trying to build a large membership but hopes to reach all associations, large and small, national and regional, which share these concerns, and through these associations, their members.[13]

PAAC alternated meetings in New York and Washington, and costs were paid out of pocket. By July 1970 PAAC had attracted the following individual sponsors, most of them with national, if not international, reputations:

---

[12]   "Back to the Old Drawing Board," *PAX*, no. 3 (January 1971): 1.

[13]   "Peace, Everybody's Business; Nobody's Job," *PAX*, no. 1 (April 1970): 3.

- Kenneth Boulding, University of Colorado
- Norman Cousins, President, World Association of World Federalists
- Morton Deutsch, Columbia University
- Jerome Frank, Johns Hopkins University
- Arthur Goldberg, former US Ambassador to the United Nations
- Ernest Gruening, former US Senator
- Seymour Halpern, US Congressman
- Vance Hartke, US Senator
- Mark Hatfield, US Senator
- Theodore Hesburgh, President, Notre Dame University
- Roger Hilsman, Columbia University
- Townsend Hoopes, former Undersecretary, US Air Force
- Arthur Larson, Director, Rule of Law, Research Center Duke University
- Harold Lasswell, Yale University
- Paul Moore, Jr., Bishop Coadjutor, New York Diocese
- Hans Morganthau, Director, Center for the Study of American Foreign Policy, University of Chicago
- Henry Reuss, US Congressman
- Frederick Schuman, Portland State University
- Gordon Sherman, President, Midas International Corporation
- David Shoup, former Commandant, US Marine Corps
- Gloria Steinem, *New York Magazine*
- Alan Westin, Columbia University
- Jerome Wiesner, Provost, MIT
- Harold Willens, Business Men's Educational Fund
- Herbert York, University of California

In a *Playboy* interview in May 1970, Senator Hartke noted:

When we speak of a Department of Peace we are discussing the means by which the idealism of the United States can be reconciled—not compromised—with the exigencies of political life.... A nation must defend those interests that are essential to its survival; but the creation of a Department of Peace will symbolize our realization that first among those interests is the preservation of the nation's sense of moral responsibility.

The effort was fundamentally practical. As Liebman argued:

This is a nation, not of philosophers, but of inventors, engineers, builders: a working people. Through some terrible displacement of energy, a kind of cosmic computer error, a whole generation of Americans has been programmed to work for war, and being the kind of people they are, have produced the biggest and best there is. It would strike de Tocqueville as typically American to perfect a doom machine and refer to it as "hardware."

What are the chances of harnessing this innovative, pragmatic national genius, and the resources of the richest country in the world on behalf of peace? A lot of doves don't believe that a government persuaded by its own ideological cant, and convinced of its own military invincibility, will support an office that challenges both. They insist that a federal peace agency would be no more than another storefront behind which the corrupt establishment could do business as usual; private peace efforts would be co-opted; the triumph of double-think would be complete.

What's the alternative?

We are trying to halt a juggernaut in our spare time, with marginal energy and with our own money; between sales meetings, trips to the orthodontist, weddings, funerals, lectures on drug abuse, balancing the bank statement, coaching Little League, preparing for bar exams and mowing early hay—and while simultaneously serving on the school board and the civil rights committee and saving the environment. Quite a job for even the most dedicated volunteer brigade. It's discouraging to remember than on Monday morning, after our march disperses, thousands of employees will show up in the Pentagon (decent husbands and fathers all, with their own problems, crab grass, confused kids, etc.) ready to put in another productive week in the service of the juggernaut; paid by us.

Supposing we are able, with our smudgy mimeographed appeals to conscience and our amateur guitar music, to get together politically, the job will still be just begun. We have to dismantle the juggernaut, piece by piece, and then to construct effective new machinery with which to deal with the real hostilities of a real world. . . .

Our commitment is the wedge, the fulcrum, on which the power of government can be deployed for peace.[14]

By that time PAAC had spent about $10,000, most of that in services contributed by fewer than twenty members. For most

---

[14] "A Very Simple Proposition," *PAX*, no. 2 (July 1970): 1–2.

peace activists of the time, opposing the war in Vietnam was more pressing than establishing an ongoing peace department.

Back to the Drawing Board: The 92nd Congress and After

Alas, the Peace Act died with the adjournment of the 91st Congress in January 1971:

> No hearings were held, and all of us who supported the legislation are disappointed that it did not receive fuller consideration, though few of us were so sanguine as to expect early enactment.

> "May you live in interesting times," says the old Chinese curse, and the months that followed the introduction of the Peace Act were wildly interesting. While millions struggled in the terrestrial mud, four Americans strolled on the moon. Proponents of the Act saw the NASA triumph as a spectacular example of what this country can do when it commits its best brains, its superior technology, and its vast wealth to a challenge....

> Our inability to spread the word far enough, fast enough, is the simple explanation for inattention to the Peace Act. The normal problems of any education-and-promotion program were vastly complicated by the pace of events in these "interesting times," and with our exertions it's unlikely that we reached more than one of every thousand Americans.[15]

---

[15]   "Back to the Old Drawing Board," *PAX*, no. 3 (January 1971): 1.

In the process, of course, criticisms were voiced. Among them was the idea that the Secretary of State could adequately fulfill the functions of a Secretary of Peace. However,

> the existence of nations implies the existence of national interests, and in the event of conflicting interests, every nation has a man charged with seeing to it that his people don't get pushed around.... For the present, and for as far as we can see into the future, there ARE American interests that can and must be protected, honorably promoted, actively pursued, and the State Department is the office to single-mindedly consider those interests. The cynical response to American policy which has been described as "credibility gap" is invoked when we require the Secretary to dissemble, to call national interest by some other name.[16]

It might of course happen that the Secretaries of State and Peace would be opposed in some specific matters. What then? Well, what? There's nothing new about dissension, even at the cabinet level. Of course the policy-making importance of the cabinet varies from one administration to another, but cabinet posts are *always* visible. Liebman continues:

> Then, say the critics, you want this Department primarily as a rallying symbol for the peace movement? Not primarily, we reply [noting that there is a] cogent case for the administrative aspect, for the clearer planning and more efficient administration of our scattered peace programs. We intend and expect this to be a working office. However, in a country where almost every high

---

[16] "Back to the Old Drawing Board," *PAX*, no. 3 (January 1971): 2.

school band is costumed as for the Charge of the Light Brigade, where churchgoers sing of Mighty Fortresses and Christian Soldiers, were almost every public festival is celebrated with military display because we have not yet invented another vocabulary for patriotism—in that kind of country, the symbolic value of a Peace Department should not be quickly dismissed.[17]

On a more mundane level, since the Peace Act had expired, the PAAC could no longer call itself the Peace Act Advisory Council. It dissolved and reincorporated under a new name: the Council for a Department of Peace (CODEP). PAAC leadership continued with CODEP.

The initial effort had been covered in a wide variety of publications, including, among others, *McCall's, The New York Times, True, The Federalist, The Churchman, Playboy, Washington Post, The New Republic, Dallas Morning News, Chicago Sun Times, Los Angeles Times, Journal of Conflict Resolution,* and *The San Francisco Monitor.* Notice how very many of these are mainstream publications.

Further bills were introduced into Congress as follows:

- 92nd Congress, January 3, 1971, to January 3, 1973: H.R. 208, by Representative Spark Matsunaga (D-HI), January 22, 1971; an identical bill, H.R. 6281 introduced by Representative Henry Helstoski (D-NJ), March 17, 1971; S. 2621, introduced by Senator Vance Hartke (D-IN), September 30, 1971; and an identical bill, H.R. 12600, introduced by Representative Seymour Halpern (R-NY), with fifty-six cosponsors, January 25, 1972.

---

[17]   "Back to the Old Drawing Board," *PAX*, no. 3 (January 1971): 2.

- 93rd Congress, January 3, 1973, to January 3, 1975: H.R. 1096, Representative Edward Roybal of California, January 3, 1973; H.R. 4824, Representative Spark Matsunaga of Hawaii, February 27, 1973; S. 1024, Senators Vance Hartke and Jennings Randolph.

- 94th Congress: January 3, 1975, to January 3, 1977: S. 1976, June 18, 1975, Senators Vance Hartke and Mark Hatfield introduced a bill for the Peace Academy.

Nothing came of these efforts, and CODEP ceased operation late in 1976. The final issue of *PAX* (fall 1976), the CODEP newsletter, was devoted to arguing, not for a peace department, but for the Peace Academy as proposed in S. 1976 by Senators Vance Hartke and Mark Hatfield on June 18, 1976. This is how Mary Liebman concluded that final issue:

> When the Arms Control and Disarmament Agency was set up in 1961, it had the support of Presidents Eisenhower and Kennedy, their Secretaries of Defense, Ambassadors to the U.N., the Chairmen of the Joint Chiefs of Staff, and an illustrious roster of statesmen, scientists, military experts, and legislators who agreed that traditional diplomacy and conventional military strength were not adequate to the challenge of the nuclear age. ACDA was directed to study the "scientific, economic, political, legal, social, psychological, military, and technological factors relating to the prevention of war."
>
> The momentum of this effort was lost in successive administrations. The failure of the ACDA to fulfill its

broad mandate demonstrates several truths about the nation's peace machinery. ACDA, and other peace agencies scattered through the executive branch, are underfunded, understaffed, underpublicized, and lack forceful advocacy in the White House and Congress—perhaps because they don't have enough direct access to the White House and Congress. Certainly they lack direct access to the American people, who never knew enough about the ACDA to the give the agency any political base, and never had any opportunity to monitor its performance.

The common-sense case for a Peace Academy starts with our commitment to the vastly complex task of constructing a just and secure world order. Like any other gigantic undertaking, from building a dam to landing on the moon, the job will require knowledge, methods, skills. There is a desperate shortage of dedicated professionals who possess this expertise, but people can be recruited and trained for public peace service as we recruit and train scientists, doctors, and four-star generals. Public service will be obligatory for Academy graduates. Having fulfilled that obligation, they will move on into a variety of careers—many continuing in government, with legislative, administrative, and policy-making responsibilities; others in communications, law, education, labor organizations, business; but all equipped for enlightened decision-making in an increasingly interdependent human society.

War is not a natural disaster. It is a manmade disaster, directed and carried out by ordinary people, who are hired and paid by other ordinary people, to make war. It will stop when ordinary people decide that, whatever satisfactions and rewards war have offered in the past, the risk is now too high and the return too low. Children in Boston live with anxiety; children in Belfast live with terror; children in Beirut live with despair. On their behalf we ask our government to establish a National Peace Academy. Now.

A new organization was established in 1976 to advocate for this proposal, the National Peace Academy Campaign (NPAC). As a result of those efforts, the US Institute of Peace finally opened its doors in 1986. It is an open question, however, whether or not the institute is the kind of organization that Mary Liebman and so many others had worked for. In an article originally published in *Z Magazine* in the July/August 1990 issue, Sarah Diamond and Richard Hatch remark:

> Under scrutiny, the supposed peace research sponsored by the federally funded U.S. Institute of Peace (USIP) looks more like the study of new and potential means of aggression, though less in the conventional military realm and more in the vein of trade embargoes, economic austerity programs, and electoral intervention.[18]

A Proposed Declaration of Purpose for the Peace Act

The following paragraphs summarize the Declarations of

---

[18]   The full article is available at the *Z Magazine* website: https://zcomm.org/zmagazine/operation-peace-institute-by-site-administrator/.

Purpose accompanying each of the bills presented to the 91st and 92nd Congresses. Mary Liebman published them in *PAX: The Peace Act Exchange*, 2, no. 1 (February 1972): 2.

―――――∞◦∞―――――

"The Government of The United States is empowered by our Constitution to take all measures which will insure domestic tranquility, provide for the common defense, and promote the general welfare of the people. The Government of the United States is committed by the Kellogg-Briand Pact of 1929, the Nuremberg Charter of 1945, and the United Nations Charter, to a serious and continuing exertion on behalf of international peace.

"Recognizing that the security and prosperity of this Nation is endangered by conditions of disorder, threats of violence, and acts of aggression within our own society and among the nations of the world, it is the purpose of this Act to implement the resolve of the Constitution and to fulfill our international obligations by the establishment of a Department to advance the cause of peace and the just resolution of conflict in this Nation and throughout the world. The Department of Peace shall ...

"– continually advise the President with respect to the prospects for peace in this nation and abroad;

"– develop and recommend to the President appropriate plans and programs designed to minimize the use of armed force in the resolution of conflict;

"– exercise leadership at the direction of the President in co-ordination of all activities of this government which may advance the cause of peace;

"– cooperate with the governments of other nations, and

with national and international organizations, public and private, in the creation of institutions which will strengthen the cause of peace;

"– devise and direct educational programs which will further among the people an understanding of the true meaning of peace, and support research into the nature, cause, and prevention of conflict; for this purpose an Education and Research Division shall be established;

"– facilitate the exchange of ideas, and increase the opportunity for relationships of friendship and respect among our own people, and between the people of this and other countries; for this purpose a Human Encounter Division shall be established;

"– encourage and extend programs to secure economic conditions conducive to lasting peace through: the maintenance of a sound peace-based economy in this nation; the expansion of trade and commerce on terms of mutual benefit; responsible stewardship for the natural resources on which human life depends; and the direction of those resources into a better quality of life for all men; for this purpose a Division of Peace Economics shall be established:

"– support all efforts on the part of governments and private groups to promulgate concepts of justice and rules of law under which the interests of all men shall be protected and reconciled, and all programs which endeavor to extend to international relationships those ethical and moral principles upon which laws are based; for this purpose a Division of Human Equity shall be established."

Waging Peace

Charlie Keil

I am adding this spring 2016 introduction to "Waging Peace" (originally published on the web October 1, 2001) because fifteen years later it seems more obvious each day that time is running out on our species, *Humo ludens collaborans.* Our humor, playfulness, and seemingly infinite capacities for intense collaboration have been celebrated in thousands of very different cultures over many tens of thousands of years, and, so far, it is only the "civilization and progress" of the past few millennia that has led us into the temptations of warfare, empire, status, and power-seeking through the manipulations of ever more complex technologies. Now our technologies of destruction (bio, chemical, nuclear, digital, and other nanotech weapons of mass destruction on the way) have so outpaced our moral and political capacities that going any further with our current modes of production, our normal economic and political agendas, will extinguish many vertebrate species including our own, forever.

> we tied in korea
> we lost in Vietnam
> been losing ever since
> do you understand?

This four-line poem makes one point: war is obsolete.

The Bernie Sanders campaign makes many other points, over and over again: that we and all the peoples of the world require much greater economic and social justice and a profound restoration of environmental sanity in order to create conditions of world peace and roll back climate change.

If subsequent rounds of terrorism here hit a few nuclear power stations and Chernobylize significant portions of East and West Coasts, *if* more *bio-weapons and different kinds of bioengineered bio-weapons* are released, and *if* the West keeps acting out the scenarios of retaliation as scripted by terrorists, then this country will not have the resources to help solve the world's problems even if it should eventually summon up the common sense, common decency, and courage to do so.

Waging Peace

I'm all for enduring freedoms here and worldwide. I'm for finite human justice, "patient justice" (Bush) as a path toward peace, and Gaia's Infinite Justice too. I want terrorists, war criminals, and mass murderers of all sorts turned over to a world court for trials and punishment. Sometimes I can think I'm on the same page with key slogans in a Bush speech, and the shifts in overall administration rhetoric often seem to be seeking a better direction, a proper multilateral response, an alliance that will work. I would really like to feel unified with my fellow Americans and with world citizens who are seeking justice, freedom, freedom from fear, peace, and democracy—all the good goals.

But it's called "America's New War" in the corporate-sponsored media campaign. War of some kind is just assumed to be the obvious response to this terrorism. It is not.

None of the possibly good reasons for air strikes or sending in an army or police force—to stop cleansing or genocide or to stop fascist aggression—can be applied here. And, perhaps more important, none of the bad or greedy reasons for war apply either.

This time we can NOT protect our oil supplies in the Middle East by going to war. This time we can NOT revive our economy and world capitalism by going to war. This time we can NOT win or control "the enemy," claim enemy turf, or destroy the enemy's capacity for violence with conventional or unconventional warfare. They are not located in any one place. They are few and far between. Many small needles are in many very big haystacks. What if we got super lucky and hit Sammy B. Laden and his entire gang with the very first bomb dropped somewhere? Instant Martyrs will inspire generations of terrorists. His tapes will be dubbed and distributed widely. Even if the very first miraculous mission by special forces brought a bunch of terrorists back alive in some helicopters for a fair trial? We still could not possibly win a war against terrorism.

The suicidal and nonsuicidal maniacs are spread around. Could be anywhere. Are everywhere. They don't need orders or a plan from a center anywhere. They need $3 box cutters. They don't need to know how to take off or land. They need $100 to bribe the guy who gives licenses to carry hazardous materials in a truck. Under present circumstances any terrorists caught or rounded up can easily be replaced. And with a war of any kind, many more terrorists are likely to be produced—and not only from a few dozen countries in the Muslim world. It only takes two (Tim M. and his friend), or a few pals, or even just one person home alone (Ted K.), a tiny splinter group from a Chinese cult or a Japanese clique, a few smart skinheads in Dresden or Budapest, an angry little cell or faction within any one of almost two hundred nationalist states or within any of the more than a thousand ethnic groups oppressed within those nationalist states: angry Kurds, angry Tutsi, angry East Timorese, angry Basques, angry any one person anywhere.

Any one person on the planet who has seen so much suffering and injustice that those delicate threads of compassion that bind us all to each other have snapped can devise a scheme for bringing down a building or destroying a communications center or poisoning a water supply or turning an area the size of Pennsylvania into a nuclear desert or spreading a bacteria that can destroy 20 percent of humanity—or 90 percent of humanity or 100 percent of humanity. Why would someone who is committing suicide care whether he is taking six thousand people, six million people, or six billion people with him? Ecology. "Eco" means home. We are now living in one home, and if one of us goes crazy and/or gets angry and/or has the wrong interpretation of a holy book, it can hurt us all.

Once you put yourself to sleep counting angries jumping over security fences, then you can wake up and start counting crazies. And when you have finished with angry-man scenarios and crazy-man scenarios, think of the angry and crazy women who can bring down half the sky more easily than men. Would a cute, blonde farm-girl-looking pilot have any trouble renting a crop duster for her anthrax tomorrow? Plus religious fanatics. And don't forget accidents, the random perversity of animate and inanimate objects.

War won't work anymore at all, and terrorism will work better and better with every passing day because of one very simple fact: increasing complexity.

Let me repeat it a few times for emphasis because it is a fact that doesn't seem to be registering quickly enough with the Overcentralized Intelligence Agency and our leaders.

War won't work anymore at all, and terrorism will work better and better with every passing day because of one very simple fact: increasing complexity.

War won't work anymore at all, and terrorism will work better and better with every passing day because of one very simple fact: increasing complexity.

The system has become too complex, too intertwined, and too vulnerable in more than a million ways. You, whoever you are reading this, have already imagined in your head at least two or three ways in which one person acting alone, or just a few people acting together, could produce a more horrible day for the United States than what happened on September 11.

Once the global economy, global communications, global resource depletions, global invention of new chemicals, global productions of new bacteria, new viruses, new prions, new technologies for spreading everything to everyone (make that two simple facts: increasing complexity and lots more bioengineered bad stuff) have gotten to the stage we reached on September 11, all the big-tech war machinery is worse than useless. Box cutters or bare hands—or a single piece of disinformation or misinformation, or a wandering gene, or a nasty bacterium—can do amazing damage as the impact ripples through the complex, intertwined system (ever more filled with bioengineered bad stuff). All the B-1, B-2, B-3 bombers and aircraft carriers in the world can't stop it. Nor can ground troops.

What can we do? We can declare peace anytime. Enact peace. Be peace. Each of us. Now. And as we transform ourselves, we transform the military-industrial-oil-based economy into a peacetime sustainable economy. Some will do this out of idealism or religious obligation or from spiritual awakening. Others will do this out of pragmatism and realpolitik. Machiavellian motivation to seize whatever power remains might easily motivate peace work at this time. Honest patriotism and just wanting to do something could bring millions of Americans to a peace and justice plan of action. Because war just won't work anymore. Too big, too expensive, too cumbersome, too much collateral damage, too much environmental devastation, and too much trauma passed down the generations with bad physical and mental health effects on grandchildren who might become terrorists fifty years from now.

War won't work against terrorism. Peace will. Waging peace will create jobs. Waging peace will pump up the economy. Waging peace will bring European and Japanese investors back to America. Waging peace will make friends and trading partners for America throughout the globe. Waging peace will put capital to work in productive, life-affirming, sustainable ways that solve the major problems of our times. Waging war in this new era does the opposite of all this. Loss of jobs. Loss of overseas investors. Loss of capital. Loss of trading possibilities. Rippling losses in all directions. We can do comprehensive peace work in place of a stupid war that can only be a loss-loss-loss-loss situation.

Waging peace will stop terrorism the only way it can be stopped, by giving everyone a minimum but absolutely necessary faith in the way things work: mass murderers will be brought to justice, the biggest thieves will be caught, justice will be witnessed in the light of public space, and people will be able to "keep the faith" just enough not to want to commit suicide while taking a lot of people with them. Probably the rich will still be rich, the poor will still be poor and always with us, and the size of the middle classes will continue to fluctuate in a sustainable peacetime global economy. But we can't afford obscene wealth and conspicuous consumption anymore because it incites terrorism. And we can't afford grinding poverty and famines anymore because it incites terrorism.

No guarantees here. But we can try to heal the angries, soothe the crazies, defuse fanaticism, and pray that no serious accidents will happen as the already released pollutants combine in new ways, as the already released radiation speeds up mutation, as the already bioengineered creatures make their way through the environment and start shaping an evolutionary process that used to be Gaia's alone.

We need about $225–250 billion a year to give the world exactly what it wants (see below), to actually save the world, to end terrorism, to move into sustainable economics and a balanced ecology, and to have the broad parameters for peace and justice in place.

Selling off half of GE's stock value (five hundred billion dollars) could pay for it the first year.

Coca-Cola is capitalized at around $110 to $130 billion. Pepsi is worth $60 billion. Cash in the sugar-water kings to pay for the second year? Things could go much better.

Or a billionaires club of fifty of the world's richest individuals could contribute $200 billion each year, and they would all still be billionaires next year.

Or we could ask each country with a big military budget to give the world a third of their military spending. They would still have $550 billion to waste on useless war machinery and armies that no longer have anywhere to go.

One way or another, I know we can find the money.

We have to find it all because waging peace *must* be comprehensive on all fronts. Leaving one world problem unsolved will eventually cause serious terrorism.

Two decades ago (1997) the World Game Institute identified

eighteen fronts and proposed eighteen detailed strategies, putting an annual price tag on each to achieve "What the World Wants." It's a finite and doable list, and I think every country in the United Nations would be happy to help; they'd be embarrassed not to.

The contradictions, the laws of supply and demand, the invisible hand of the market, the evening news, a very vivid, practical and completely nonutopian vision of how happy people would be reforesting, saving topsoil, feeding all the children—it all tells me the same thing: everything points toward comprehensive peace-making now or maybe never.

Here's a short list of problems and very approximate costs to solve them as of 1997:

	Action Taken	**Cost**
1	Eliminate starvation and malnourishment	19 billion per year for ten years
2	Provide basic health care for all not currently served, childhood immunization, including iodine deficiency, AIDS prevention and control	15 billion per year for ten years
3	Eliminate inadequate housing and homelessness	21 billion per year for ten years
4	Provide clean and abundant water	10 billion per year for ten years
5	Eliminate illiteracy	5 billion a year for ten years
6	Increase energy efficiency	33 billion per year for ten years
7	Increase renewable energy	17 billion per year for ten years
8	Debt management	30 billion per year for ten years
9	Stabilize population	11 billion per year for ten years

10	Preserving cropland	24 billion per year for ten years
11	Reversing deforestation	7 billion per year for ten years
12	Reverse ozone depletion[19]	5 billion per year for twenty years
13	Stop acid rain	8 billion per year for ten years
14	Reverse global warming	8 billion per year for twenty years
15	Removal of landmines	2 billion per year for ten years
16	Refugee relief	5 billion per year for ten years
17	Eliminating nuclear weapons	7 billion a year for ten years
18	Building democracy	2 billion a year for ten years

Note: You could do fifteen or eighteen for less than it costs to build one B-2 bomber or for less than one-half of what the United States spends on perfume each year or for 0.025 percent of the world's annual military expenditures.[19]

Are we serious about Enduring Freedom and "patient justice" or not?

Spring 2016

At this writing, April 20, 2016, I don't see any need to apologize for any mistakes or missed estimates made fifteen years ago in the "Waging Peace" article of October 2001. Finally, in this election

---

[19]   This list came from the World Game Institute over a decade ago. As far as we can tell, the list is no longer up. The World Game Institute certainly exists, but under a different name: O. S. Earth (http://www.osearth.com/).

year, we are witnessing millions of young Americans waking up to the facts, connecting the dots, and realizing that all of humanity may not have a future if we stay on the warpath.

Fortunately, the solution is as clear as the situation is dire:

1. Phase out warring, and negotiate disarmament with inspections.
2. Phase in policing, and open source intelligence.
3. Set an example for the democracies of the world by
   a. starting a very small peace department that supplies multiple peace options for every situation, big, small, medium, or global; and
   b. supporting the formation of a Global Organization of Democracies (GOOD) that meets year-round, one nation, one representative, one vote.
4. Pursue purposes and politics based upon two principles:
   a. self-determination of peoples; and
   b. democratic confederalism within existing borders.

Resolution for a Department of Peace

Charlie Keil

Whereas reasoning people of conscience have long condemned wars;

Whereas wars waste humanity and the Creation and are now squandering the equivalent of trillions of dollars globally;

Whereas many of the growing and spreading technologies called weapons of mass destruction (biological, chemical, and nuclear) can now be wielded to devastating effect by a single individual;

Whereas many previous treaties meant to end wars have been ignored or forgotten;

Whereas the constitutional requirements for a congressional declaration of war have been evaded many, many times since World War II;

Be it resolved, that the Department of Peace be established to

1. develop and recommend to the President appropriate plans, policies, and programs designed to foster peace; and

2. cooperate with the governments of other nations in research and planning for the peaceful resolution of international conflict and encourage similar action by private institutions.

The first "whereas" builds upon rights to "reason and conscience" as articulated in Article One of the Universal Declaration of Human Rights.

The second "whereas" gives a capital letter to "Creation" as used by Pope Francis in his recent *Encyclical on Climate Change and Inequality*.

The third "whereas" could be expanded to add "mechanical" to bio, chemo, or nukes, or it could specify "drones," RPGs (rocket-propelled grenades), nanontech, or digital sabotage as further technological advances that make the world ever more dangerous and war totally obsolete as a means to any good end. Our science and tech make everyone increasingly vulnerable to everyone else in this increasingly complex world. Time to simplify and secure whatever can be secured by nuclear and other disarmament and inspection processes.

Just what could the Department of Peace do? Aaron Voldman has the beginnings of an answer:

We're often asked, "If a Department of Peace existed, how would it respond to the situation in Iraq?" First, during the pre-war phase, the department would've worked to prevent war by researching, analyzing, and recommending nonviolent solutions and strategies to resolve the conflict. Then, during the war, it would've provided peace builders to assist the military in maintaining order. Finally, during the post-war phase, a Department of Peace would've assisted in reconstruction and reconciliation, proactively working to quell disputes before they reached a violent climax.[20]

---

[20]   Aaron Voldman, "The Vietnam corollary," *Bulletin of the Atomic Scientists* (August 30, 2007): http://thebulletin.org/rebirth-anti-nuclear-weapons-movement/vietnam-corollary.

Appendix:
List of Selected Peace Organizations

Wikipedia has a page listing entries on more than 2000 peace organizations: https://en.wikipedia.org/wiki/Category:Peace_organizations

A. J. Muste Memorial Institute, 339 Lafayette Street, New York, NY 10012 • phone: 212.533.4335 • web: http://www.ajmuste.org • email: info@ajmuste.org

Alliance for Peacebuilding, 1800 Massachusetts Ave N W #401, Washington, DC 20036 • phone: 202.822.2047 • web: http://www.allianceforpeacebuilding.org • email: afp-info@allianceforpeacebuilding.org

Beyond Nuclear, 6930 Carroll Ave. Suite 400, Tacoma Park, MD 20912 • phone: 301.270.2209 • web: http://www.beyondnuclear.org • email: info@beyondnuclear.org

Catholic Worker, 36 East First St., New York, NY 10003; phone 212.254.1640 • web: http://www.catholicworker.org/index.html • email: michael_finger@hotmail.com

CodePink, PO Box 475142, San Francisco, CA 94147 • web: http://www.codepink.org • email: info@codepink.org

Fellowship of Reconciliation, PO Box 271, Nyack, NY 10960 • phone: 845-358-4601 • web: http://forusa.org

Global Network Against Weapons and Nuclear Power in Space, PO Box 652, Brunswick, ME 04011 • phone: 207.443.9502 • web: http://www.space4peace.org • email: globalnet@mindspring.com

Iraq Veterans Against the War, PO Box 3565, New York, NY 10008 • phone: 646.723.0989 • web: http://www.ivaw.org

Mayors for Peace, 1-5 Nakajima-cho, Naka-ku, Hiroshima 730-0811 Japan • phone: +81-82-242-7821 • web: http://www.mayorsforpeace.org • email: mayorcon@pcf.city.hiroshima.jp

National Campaign for a Peace Tax Fund, 2121 Decatur Place NW, Washington, DC 20008 • phone: 202.483.3751 • web: http://www.peacetaxfund.org • email: Jack@peacetaxfund.org

National War Tax Resistance Coordinating Committee, PO Box 150553, Brooklyn, NY 11215 • phone: 718.768.3420 • web: http://nwtrcc.org • email: nwtrcc@nwtrcc.org

Nuclear Age Peace Foundation, PMB 121, 1187 Coast Village Rd. Suite 1, Santa Barbara, CA 93108 • phone: 805.965.3443 • web: https://www.wagingpeace.org

Peace Action Education Fund, 8630 Fenton St. Suite 524, Silver Spring, MD 20910 • phone: 301.565.4050 • web: http://www.peace-action.org

Peace Alliance, 1616 P St. NW Suite 100, Washington, DC 20036 • phone: 202.684.2553 • web: http://peacealliance.org • email: info@thepeacealliance.org

War Resisters League, 339 Lafayette St. New York, NY 10012 • phone: 212.228.0450 • web: https://www.warresisters.org • email: wrl@warresisters.org

World Beyond War, AFGJ 225 E. 26th St. #1, Tucson, AZ 85713 • web: http://worldbeyondwar.org • email: info@actionnetwork.org

About the Authors

William Benzon has published *Visualization: The Second Computer Revolution* (with Richard Friedhoff), *Beethoven's Anvil: Music in Mind and Culture*, and numerous articles on literature, cognitive science, and culture. He maintains a blog, New Savanna (http://new-savanna.blogspot.com), on diverse topics. He was a conscientious objector during the final years of the war in Vietnam and did civilian service in the Chaplain's Office at The Johns Hopkins University.

Charlie Keil has been making music and writing about music and society from the 1960s to the present: *Urban Blues*, *Tiv Song*, *Polka Happiness*, *My Music*, *Music Grooves*, *Bright Balkan Morning*, *Born to Groove*, and *Polka Theory* (forthcoming). A conscientious objector to war since age seventeen, he's hoping to see world peace in his lifetime.

Mary Liebman (1923–2011) found her way from rural Illinois to the writings of Benjamin Rush on the Department of Peace. Without credentials or formal training but with a manual typewriter and countless cigarettes, she became a respected public voice promoting the idea from her kitchen table during the Vietnam War and beyond.

Benjamin Rush (1756–1813) was a Philadelphia physician, a founder of Dickinson College, the father of American psychiatry, an abolitionist, a member of the Continental Congress, and a signer of the *Declaration of Independence*. He also taught chemistry, medical theory, and clinical practice at the University of Pennsylvania.

Frederick Schuman (1904–1981) was educated at the University of Chicago and taught there for ten years. He then taught at Williams College for thirty-two years, where he became the Woodrow Wilson Professor of Government. Upon retiring from Williams, he moved to Oregon, where he became Professor of Political Science at Portland State University. Among his many publications are *War and Diplomacy in the French Republic*, *The Nazi Dictatorship*, *The Commonwealth of Man*, *Russia Since 1917*, and *International Politics* (7th ed., 1969).